LENT

through the

LITTLE THINGS

NOW AVAILABLE!

the LITTLE THINGS

Companion Journal

Get your <u>FREE</u> download

(printable or fillable PDF) at:

https://www.lindahanstra.com/lenten-companion-journal

LENT

through the

LITTLE THINGS

encountering Jesus

in life's ordinary moments

LINDA HANSTRA

MiWoods Press
Lent through the Little Things
Copyright © 2023 Linda Hanstra

Cover design/Illustration: Linda Hanstra/Canva
Interior design: Linda Hanstra
Printed in the United States of America
ISBN: 979-8-9876661-1-1

Thanks be to you, our Lord Jesus Christ,
for all the benefits which you have given us,
for all the pains and insults which you have borne for us.
Most merciful Redeemer,
Friend and Brother,
may we know you more clearly,
love you more dearly,
and follow you more nearly,
day by day. Amen.

(St. Richard of Chichester, 1197-1223)

Lent through the Little Things

Encountering Jesus in Life's Ordinary Moments

Week One: We Begin

Week Two: Around the House

Week Three: Out and About

Week Four: Nature Walk

Week Five: Infrastructure

Week Six: People

Week Seven: Holy Week

Introduction

Lent: a time to give up, take on, and tune in

Growing up in a Protestant church, I wasn't aware of the liturgical church calendar, much less the season of Lent. I became vaguely aware during my public high school days when my Catholic friends would mention something they "gave up for Lent." In the following years, during college and beyond, my awareness of, and eventually my participation in the practices of Lent grew.

I now know that during the season of Lent–the 40 days before Easter–Christians are called to focus their minds on and make space for remembering God's great gift of salvation, Jesus. Though not biblically rooted, early church leaders designed the church calendar and these practices in order to establish rhythms and rituals of worship. What began in the Catholic and Orthodox traditions has gradually moved into many Protestant churches as well.

In the church I attend, we recognize the season of Lent by adorning the space with liturgical decors, such as purple vestments, banners, and tablecloths; by extinguishing a candle each of the six weeks leading up to Good Friday; and by "putting away our Alleluias," in word and in song, until Easter Sunday.

Though not required in a legalistic way, our pastor encourages personal practices on the weekdays as well. In order to decrease distractions and serve as a daily reminder of Christ's ultimate sacrifice, many Christians *give up* something (e.g. a vice or worldly pleasure) or *take on* something (e.g. a holy or healthy habit). These days, among my friends and even in my household, I often hear comments like these during those six weeks before Easter:

"Did you give up something for Lent?"

"I've heard you should actually take something on."

"I'm giving up *chocolate." (*insert any other loved food or drink)

"I gave up Facebook for Lent."

"I'm committing to a daily walk.

"I took on morning meditation."

The idea of giving up or taking on is that through physical denial or practice, our minds will be drawn to acknowledge our sinfulness, move toward repentance, and accept the forgiveness we receive through Jesus' sacrificial death on the cross.

Every year I have good intentions of doing just that. I've given things up and taken things on. But those changes don't always change my focus. Life gets in the way, and I soon realize days or weeks have gone by, and all I've thought about is how many days until I can have chocolate again and who's coming for Easter dinner. With a twinge of guilt (but the promise of grace), I approach Holy Week and all it means to me. And I promise to do better next year.

It is with those thoughts in mind that I approached these meditations. I've often wondered how Jesus escaped me when I had good intentions of finding him. If I only had simple reminders throughout my day of his presence, perhaps I could make his nearness more real to me.

We know that Jesus, Son of God, is always with us, even when we may not acknowledge his presence. He's there, and if we only *tune in,* we can't miss him.

I designed these meditations to help us on our Lenten journey to the cross. Each week we will focus on a different aspect of our everyday surroundings to remind us of Jesus' presence.

Week 1 (days 1-4) - The Journey Begins
Week 2 (days 5-10) - Around the House
Week 3 (days 11-16) - Out and About
Week 4 (days 17-22) - Nature Walk
Week 5 (days 23-28) - Infrastructure
Week 6 (days 29-34) - People
Week 7 (35-40) - Holy Week

This book is a guide. It's not a manual, a pass/fail exam, or a ticket to salvation. God's grace and forgiveness are free to anyone who believes. I hope that the daily readings, reminders to tune in, and prayers will guide us to that truth over and over again.

Although anytime is acceptable to read your daily meditation, doing so in the morning will increase your mindfulness throughout the day. Each day's reading should only take a couple of minutes. If you miss a day (we all know life happens), you can skip it or double up your readings. There are no readings for Sundays, as those are traditionally not a part of the 40 days of Lent. Instead, allow yourself to bask in God's love on Sundays. I like taking a walk, listening to music, reading a good book, or spending time with my family. You should do what is meaningful to you.

Each reading begins with a short passage from the Bible. Verses are quoted from the New Revised Standard Version (Updated Edition), unless otherwise noted. As you complete the readings, follow the suggestions to "Take Notice," and read the daily prayer, you will begin looking for Jesus (and finding him!) in your everyday surroundings. His presence in your Lenten journey will keep you *tuned in* to the wonders of his grace!

Consider this your invitation to join me on this walk to the cross, as we meet Jesus in the ordinary "Little Things" of our everyday lives.

week one:

We Begin

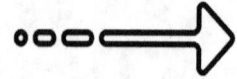

wednesday

Ashes

All go to one place, all are from the dust, and all turn to dust again. Ecclesiastes 3:20
Jesus said to [Martha], "I am the resurrection and the life. Those who believe in me, even though they die, will live." John 11:25

Many churches, Protestant and Catholic alike, observe Ash Wednesday. Although I didn't grow up with the tradition, it has become a very meaningful day of worship for me. After a busy hump day at work, we hustle off to the simple soup supper our church hosts before the service. After a brief time of fellowship over dinner, the congregation moves over to the sanctuary, where we sing a few pensive songs, pray, read scripture, and hear a brief message. Then we walk forward for what is called the imposition of ashes.

Our pastor presses her thumb against my forehead, and with ash, she smudges the shape of a cross. I hear those familiar words, "You are dust, and to dust you shall return." It's a sobering thought. And for years, I walked away from that service with a reminder of my sins–a black blot on my face–and my mortality, as those words replayed in my mind.

But there was something very different about Ash Wednesday, 2021. We had not seen our church family in person for months. During the winter, as the pandemic raised its ugly head yet again, it forced us to worship at home, watching church on the livestream. And then, in the bleak, late-winter, we received an invitation: Please join us for our "Ash Wednesday Drive-thru" service.

We warmed up the car and drove to church. There was no soup supper. No time of fellowship. No wandering into the sanctuary.

What we found instead were the smiling faces of our pastor, our youth director, and her husband, greeting us at our car windows, ashes in hand. We received our smudged crosses. We received the words reminding us we would someday return to dust. But we received so much more.

Behind the ashes and that stark reminder were smiles, joy, and laughter. It was so good to reunite for even a moment with those dear ones.

As we enter Ash Wednesday, the beginning of our somber journey to the cross, let us remember our sins. Let us not forget our mortality and the fleeting nature of the Earth we inhabit. But let's also remember that this journey has a destination like no other. As we walk alongside Jesus in our everyday lives, we do so with the confidence that he will wash away that smudge in the end. Through his ultimate sacrifice on the cross and triumph over death, we can look forward to a heavenly reunion with our loved ones and saints that have gone before us, filled with smiles, joy, and laughter.

Take notice

If an Ash Wednesday service is available to you, attend one today. If not, consider driving by a cemetery, touch your own forehead and say these words to yourself: "You are dust, and to dust you shall return."

Prayer

Lord Jesus, thank you for my life. Help me live fully in the knowledge of your saving grace and the eternal joy to come when my days on Earth are done. Amen.

thursday

Ping it

When you search for me, you will find me; if you seek me with all your heart. Jeremiah 29:13

The older I get, the more I find myself searching for things.

"Where did I put that jacket?"

"Why aren't my keys in my purse?"

And the most common: "What happened to my phone?"

I now have a solution! My watch, which is almost always on my wrist, connects to my phone. When I misplace my phone, I just tap the "phone" icon on my watch. Then, "PING-PING-PING!" I can hear my phone in another room, under the couch cushion, or sitting in plain sight–though somehow elusive to me–on the kitchen counter.

Another brilliant invention is the trackable tag you can attach to your valuables, like purses, keys, or backpacks. When used for its intended purpose, this little device can help you track down lost bags and luggage. It makes the search for your valuables much easier.

In this season of Lent, we are searching for something or someone more valuable than our luggage or phones. We're searching for Jesus.

He often seems elusive. We can't see him, so we wonder if he's really there. Or we believe he's there but is out of reach. We want and need his presence but just can't tap into it. If only we could "PING" him with the touch of a button.

Yet, he promised he's always with us. In Matthew 28:20, after telling his disciples to go and make more disciples out of all the nations, he gave them these reassuring words: *"And surely I am with you always, to the very end of the age."* As followers of Jesus, we can claim that promise as well.

We just need reminders to reach out to him. And they are all around us. When I see, hear, smell, taste, and feel the ordinary things he's blessed me with, a picture or metaphor might come to mind. These reminders of his presence, along with faith in his promises, help me to meet Jesus right where I am.

Over the coming weeks, as we take notice of these reminders together, we will find him. We'll see him around the house and in nature. We'll catch glimpses of him when we're out and about, and even in the foundational infrastructure of our environment, which we often ignore. Jesus will be present in the people that surround us and in our final walk to the cross during Holy Week.

There have been times when I've searched everywhere for my phone, only to realize I'm holding it to my ear and talking into it! I laugh at my distractibility and forgetfulness, and that I missed it when it was so obvious.

The next time we feel we just can't find Jesus, remember how easy it is to miss the obvious. He's present and all around us. He speaks to us through life's most extraordinary circumstances.

He also shows up daily in the most ordinary ways.

Take notice

Choose an ordinary object you often misplace (i.e. keys, phone, headphones). Whenever you pick it up today, let it remind you of Jesus' unseen presence.

Prayer

Dear Jesus, thank you for never being lost to me. Give me the assurance that you are always here, right beside me. Amen.

friday

g p s

But by the grace of God I am what I am, and his grace toward me has not been in vain. On the contrary, I worked harder than any of them, though it was not I but the grace of God that is with me. 1 Corinthians 15:10

It's hard to remember what life was like before we all had a GPS on our phones and in our cars. When we drive to a new destination, we simply look up the address, type it in, and click "Start." When our relatives want to know what time we'll arrive at their house for a visit, we can give them our ETA almost to the minute. And when we want to avoid construction or a crash on the interstate, we know in advance that we can take a detour and just how long it will take.

Thinking back, I recall earlier days without this amazing tool. I remember printing out my MapQuest directions on my home computer before leaving on a journey. We could eventually find our way by following the "right turn here" and "left turn there," but we had no way of knowing what time we'd arrive or if we'd run into any unexpected delays or detours.

Before that, there were maps and atlases. We'd study them before leaving home and have a general idea of which roads to take. Still, things weren't always clear. The road we wanted to turn on might be an unanticipated one-way street or closed due to construction. I'd scramble to open up the map and shout out directions to my husband, who would lose his patience, especially when I'd accidentally mix up my lefts and rights. "Turn left. No, I mean right!"

On our journey through Lent, we might feel we have a GPS guiding us. We know where to start—on Ash Wednesday—and where to end—on Easter Sunday. We know it will take 40 weekdays, plus six Sundays.

But in many ways, we will follow a roughly drawn map. We may experience unexpected turns and detours along the way. It's likely we'll get off course and forget the holy practices we had set out to do. As we examine our lives, we may find roadblocks that keep us from the journey.

It's comforting to know that no matter where we are along the road, Jesus has gone before us. His life is the ultimate guide for us to follow. If we keep our lives pointed toward him, we will arrive at the cross where all of our wandering and wayward paths are forgiven through his grace. Our GPS—our Grace-Pointing Savior—will guide us home.

🔍 Take notice

As you travel in your vehicle today and over the next six weeks, let your GPS remind you of the grace and mercy Jesus is pointing you toward.

🙏 Prayer

Dear Lord, keep me on your path. Turn me around when I am lost and guide me safely into your loving mercy. Amen.

saturday

Glasses and hearing aids

Listen! I am standing at the door, knocking; if you hear my voice and open the door, I will come in and eat with you, and you with me. Revelation 3:20

I was in college when I first discovered I needed glasses. My eyes had gradually become nearsighted, perhaps because of the increased amount of reading that was required. The change was so slow that I didn't even realize my sight had become blurry.

After a visit to the eye doctor, I ordered my first pair of glasses. Although I didn't mind having an extra fashion accessory, having to wear them did not excite me. I figured I had gotten by for so long without them, that wearing them would be an optional choice. If they looked good with my outfit, I'd wear them. If not, I'd leave them at home.

Then I put them on. I was amazed at the sharpness of my surroundings! Who knew the twigs on the tree branches could actually be defined by visible lines? I could read signs along the road long before I was close to them. My eyes hadn't changed, but with the glasses, everything around me became clearer. I wore them every day.

Not only do many of us rely on glasses to see well, but others need hearing aids to hear accurately. My mother wore hearing aids for years and was faithful about cleaning them, changing her batteries, and wearing them. Then her Alzheimer's set in. One hearing aid was lost for months until we found it in a small pocket in her purse. It took time for us to establish a good schedule for cleaning and battery checking.

When her hearing aids were lost or not working, it was almost impossible to communicate with her. We would resort to yelling, pantomiming, or writing things down. Still, only half of the message would get across. Getting the aids back in her ears and working again was like magic. Finally, the signals were getting through and everything became clearer.

Glasses and hearing aids are essential for a clear view and good understanding. But what about seeing God and listening to his voice? Are we getting all the signals?

Lent is a time for us to refocus and dig deeper into understanding what we believe. It's a good time to pick up a book on theology or join a Bible study group. Listening to God's voice through sacred music or podcasts of sermons can clarify the message of Scripture in new ways.

The surprising thing is, once we see and hear God more clearly, we might realize what we were missing and want to keep those "glasses" on and "hearing aids" in! The focus we experience during Lent can stay with us long after our Easter celebration and deepen our relationship with the Father, Son, and Holy Spirit throughout the year.

Take notice

Today, as you put on your glasses, contacts, or hearing aids, or see others who rely on them, remind yourself to focus your attention on the teachings of your faith.

Prayer

O, dear Lord, three things I pray: to know thee more clearly, love thee more dearly, follow thee more nearly, day by day. Amen. (Saint Richard of Chichester, 1197-1223.)

week two:

Around the House

monday

Dust and light

The true light, which enlightens everyone, was coming into the world. John 1:9

Relaxing in my peaceful living room during the evening hours, I enjoy reading a book, scrolling social media, or watching a favorite show. I've straightened things up; I can see no clutter. When the room is tidy, I feel at peace, relaxed and content with my situation.

As dusk blankets the woods that surround us with a warm glow, I gaze through the windows at our lovely backyard, hoping to get a glimpse of a deer or wild turkey. All is right with my world.

The next morning, I get up with the sun. As I go about my morning tasks, I notice the sunlight streaming through the windows. It shines a light on what was hidden the night before. My windows are spotted with dirt, dust coats the end tables and floats, particle by particle, through the air. My house is not as clean as I had envisioned the night before. In the light, the dirt comes into view.

And so it is with me. When I look at my more obvious actions, I feel great about myself and all the good things I've done. With a self-righteous attitude, I pride myself on being a good person. After all, I go to church on Sunday, read my Bible, and volunteer regularly. I'm so content with myself that, for a moment, I forget the reality of my sinfulness.

Then I open my Bible, listen to a devotional, or turn on some worship music, and the light of Jesus shines on me. I can no longer hide my sins. His words remind me I have put myself and my desires first too many times. He convicts me of my tendency to look down on others or push them away with my self-righteousness. He nudges me to see my lust for the world and greed for material things. His light brings to light my sin.

The sunlight that shines through the windows exposing the dust also forms shadows on the opposite wall. As the sun's rays hit the crossbars of the windowpanes, I see a shape form. Through the shadows, a cross appears. And once again, I am reminded of why Jesus brought his light into the world.

Our sin is not the end of the story. Instead, the light leads us to the cross and the power of forgiveness. Jesus' triumph over darkness and death is the hope we can hold on to. Hope for a world walking in darkness.

🔍 Take notice

As you look into the light today, notice the dust and dirt. Then remember and confess your sins, knowing that Jesus forgives them all if only you ask.

🙏 Prayer

Lord Jesus, thank you for bringing light into the world and for taking the dirt of our lives to the cross with you. Amen.

tuesday

Mirrors

The Lord does not look at the things people look at. People look at the outward appearance, but the Lord looks at the heart. 1 Sam. 16:7b

How many times have I looked at my face in the mirror? Or checked my "look" as I got dressed for the day?

The older I get, the less forgiving my mirror is. It reveals wrinkles around my eyes, saggy skin under my chin, and rolls under my clothes that I prefer to hide.

Still, we all rely on mirrors to show us our appearance. Our culture tells us that how we show ourselves to the world is crucial. Our *look* becomes synonymous with our sense of *self.* Without mirrors, we might reveal more than we want or put what we consider "faults" out there for everyone to see. Since mirrors reflect the image others see, they allow us to cover blemishes with a little makeup or hide a tummy roll with a baggy sweater if we choose to.

We're a people obsessed with our outward appearance, with our reflection in the mirror.

But what if we used a different tool to find our deeper faults? Or to measure our true beauty? What if we could see what's on the *inside*–our thoughts, feelings, and intentions? Jesus tells us there is a way.

The mirror we can use is the Word of God. By looking at ourselves in light of Scripture, we can see where we have fallen short. These words from the book of common prayer, often said during confession or communion, sum it up nicely: *we confess that we have sinned against you in thought, word, and deed, by what we have done, and by what we have left undone.* We can see our imperfections not only through our actions and inactions but also in our thoughts and words. Greed, jealousy, malice, and self-centeredness, to name a few, are common faults that lie within.

Thankfully, our look into this holy mirror reveals another facet of who we are. As we peer into the mirror of Scripture, we also see a marvelous creation. Both body and soul, we are made in God's image. Our beauty does not come from ourselves, but from the unconditional love of our creator Father, who formed us to carry the nature of his splendor.

Jesus came to take away our sins. The faults that lie below the surface, which we try to hide, are washed away when confessed to him. They're not covered up like blemishes under makeup, instead they are removed with no trace remaining. All we need to do is ask.

Through his grace, love, and forgiveness, God assures us we are enough. We can look into his mirror and know we are loved. And by sharing that love, his beauty will shine through us.

Take notice

As you look into the mirror today, remember that you are more than your outward appearance. Use the verse above as a reminder of how God sees you.

Prayer

Dear Jesus, help me find my true faults and to trust in your forgiveness. Then let the beauty you created in me shine through. Amen.

wednesday

Kitchen faucet

Whoever drinks the water I give them will never thirst.
Indeed, the water I give them will become in them a spring of
water welling up to eternal life. John 4:14

I wonder how many times a day we use our kitchen faucet?

We fill a pot with water to pour into the coffeemaker for our morning cup of joe. We wash our hands at the sink with a little soap and water. Rinse our dishes and wash the ones too delicate for the dishwasher. And we fill our water bottles or a glass with a drink of water when we're thirsty.

The ease with which water comes to us is a blessing we take for granted. Rarely do we give it a thought.

Imagine what it's like without running water. I'm so spoiled that the thought of having to go outside and pump a bucket of water or bring it up from the well sounds dreadful. And yet, for thousands of years, that's all people knew. Since water is crucial for survival, people did what they had to in order to get it.

Even today, there are people around the world without running water or with no source of clean, safe water. Charitable organizations and community developers provide wells and safe sources of water in these areas, while engineers work to find sustainable and culturally sensitive solutions.

Water is life-giving and life-sustaining.

In the story of the woman at the well (John 4), Jesus goes to a well in Samaria, where he meets a woman and asks her for a drink. She is surprised by his request (as it was unusual for Jews to interact with Samaritans), and her confusion mounted when Jesus began talking about "living water."

"If you knew the gift of God and who it is that asks you for a drink, you would have asked him and he would have given you living water." The woman asked how Jesus could give her this "living water" when he had no means to draw it up.

Jesus explained: *"Everyone who drinks this water will be thirsty again, but whoever drinks the water I give them will never thirst. Indeed, the water I give them will become in them a spring of water welling up to eternal life."*

The woman wanted Jesus to give her living water so she could avoid drawing water from the well every day, a task that was not only difficult but embarrassing for her because of her past. Can you blame her for wanting this water that would forever quench her thirst? I'd do the same. But after Jesus revealed himself as the Messiah, the Samaritan woman understood his meaning and ran to tell everyone in her village.

The "living water" Jesus offered to the woman at the well is for everyone, even for those of us with modern-day faucets and sinks. We may still have a thirst for water here on Earth, but our deep thirst for connection with the God who made us will only be satisfied through Jesus. All we have to do is ask our Lord to fill our cup.

 Take notice

Every time you use a faucet or drink water today, remember the "living water" Jesus offers us.

 Prayer

Lord, here is my cup. Fill me up with the living water of your love and grace. Amen.

thursday

Clutter and candles

John answered all of them by saying, "I baptize you with water, but one who is more powerful than I is coming; I am not worthy to untie the strap of his sandals. He will baptize you with the Holy Spirit and fire." Luke 3:16

I was searching for a great writing nook–a corner of the house where I could avoid distractions and feel inspired. With the kids no longer at home, I had three spare bedrooms to choose from. I opted for the one with the largest desk.

Tucked away in the corner of my daughter's old room, next to the window overlooking the garden, I found my quiet place. A corner desk with a cabinet and shelf to one side,

29

which had become a dust and clutter collector. I shoved my daughter's little trinkets aside. High School band memorabilia, a flower picture-holder with wire petals, and countless plastic 3-D puzzles from her vast collection.

I added my little basket of journals, inspirational books, and writing guides. With a couple of candles to provide warmth and a pleasing aroma, my nook was ready.

Sitting down to write, I peered out the window, searching for inspiration. But my gaze was drawn back to the shelf. Looking over the sea of clutter was the head of the plastic red robot puzzle, staring at me as if to say, "What am I doing here?" I asked him the same thing.

As we search for meaning and inspiration, sometimes God speaks to us clearly. At other times, meaningless distractions surround us, and we lose sight of our purpose. Just as the lifeless hunks of metal and plastic had blocked my view, life's distractions can interfere with our search for God.

I reached for my butane lighter and lit the candle. A white candle with three wicks. Three flames. A holy trinity of light. The flames danced in time to my music, alive with the energy that made them burn and with heat that could re-form the wax below. The same kind of heat that shaped the plastic into robot puzzles and melted the metal wire into flower petals.

Burning with purpose, a candle can remind us of our own need for reshaping and reforming. It can melt away the distractions and clear the clutter from our minds. When we look to the flame that is God–Father, Son, and Holy Spirit–

and ask him to enter our hearts, we can find our purpose and inspiration once again. Even amidst the clutter of life.

Take notice

Remove some clutter from your life today, and light a candle to remind you of the true light of Christ.

Prayer

Lord, light the flame within my heart to bring purpose to my lifeless spirit. Mold me and shape me with the warmth of your love. Amen.

friday

Rocking chair

God is our refuge and strength. A very present help in trouble.
Psalm 46:1

We have a rocking chair sitting in our guest room. But that's not where it's always been.

Its first home was our babies' nursery. It was there that I nursed my babies in the middle of the night. Where we rocked a fitful infant to sleep and read bedtime stories to our toddlers.

I can picture one baby and toddler after another, dressed in footie pajamas, with damp hair after their bath and smelling like Johnson's baby shampoo, climbing into my lap to snuggle in. Before long, with a heavy head on my shoulder, they would drift off to sleep.

As the children grew, we moved the rocking chair to our bedroom. With pinched fingers or broken hearts, the kids would climb into our laps, seeking comfort. They knew that no matter the pain, Mommy or Daddy would be there, ready to hug and console.

Eventually, the kids were too big to climb into my lap, and we moved the chair to the hallway. Serving only as a decorative piece, it became a simple reminder of the comfort it once provided.

Then, when the kids moved out and we transformed their rooms into guest rooms, the old rocking chair found a new home again in the corner of a guest room. Although it still collected dust most days, I'd occasionally rest there. When my heart ached for my children, I could sit there and be filled with fond memories of the hours spent in that chair with my babies.

Now, when our kids come to visit, they bring with them…a baby! My grandchild! His mother calms his cries, giving him the nourishment he needs, in that chair. When the baby won't settle down, *my* baby sits in that chair and rocks *his* baby to sleep. I pull my own kids' favorite books off the shelf and read stories to my grandbaby–in that chair.

That rocking chair reminds me of our heavenly Father. He waits for us to seek him for our comfort. With open arms, he asks us to bring him our pain and sorrow. He stands ready to wrap his arms around us, to hold us in his lap. He loves us with a love so deep that a parent's love pales in comparison.

Even when we *think* we don't need him–when we put him on display for decoration or shove him into a corner–he remains. Always ready and willing to hold us through the dark of night, through pain and fear. We only need to come to him and reach our arms up to him. He will pick us up, hold us close, and never let us go.

Take notice

Sit in a rocking chair or comfortable seat today and imagine your Heavenly Father's arms wrapped around you. Give him your pain and sadness, and let his love heal and comfort you.

Prayer

Heavenly Father, you have known sorrow and suffering, and promise to be with me in my pain. Hold me now in your love. Amen.

saturday

Bed

Come to me, all who labor and are heavy laden, and I will give you rest. Matthew 11:28

"Now I lay me down to sleep. *I pray the Lord my soul to keep,"* my childhood prayer began.

It was simple, as was my life. As a child, I would climb into bed, say my prayers, and quickly drift off to sleep. I rarely thought about the second, more ominous line of that prayer: *"If I should die before I wake, I pray the Lord my soul to take."*

I'm older now. And wiser. I'm more fully aware of all that could go wrong during the night, or the following day, or in the weeks to come. As I toss and turn, and flip my pillow over to the cooler side, I run through all the worries, wonders, and wrestling of the day.

We often can't wait to lie down in our beds at night for slumber, but how many times does that rest elude us? Our bodies are weary. They're yearning for sleep. Yet, sleep doesn't come.

Thankfully, we don't need to carry all of this. Jesus' words in Matthew 11 call us to let it all go. *"Come to me, all who labor and are heavy laden, and I will give you rest. Take my yoke upon you, and learn from me, for I am gentle and lowly in heart, and you will find rest for your souls. For my yoke is easy, and my burden is light"* (v. 28-30).

Jesus tells us to give him our burdens. He says he will carry them for us. Once we do, we can rest our souls. Yet, so often, we fail to give the control over to him. The tighter we hold on to our problems and worries, the more restless we become.

I think again of that childhood prayer and realize that both lines should bring us peace. Whether awake or asleep, alive or dead, our souls belong to the Lord. This means that while we're alive, we are living every day to his glory. Our worries can, and should, be placed on him. And when it's our time to meet our maker, we will still belong to him.

I have a comfortable bed. I also have a nice pillow on which to rest my head. My sheets are smooth, and my blankets are soft and warm. My bed is a comfort to me at the end of a long day.

But my true comfort? My only comfort in and beyond this world? *That I am not my own, but belong–body and soul, in life and in death–to my faithful Savior, Jesus Christ.*

(Heidelberg Catechism, Q&A #1). On those words, I can rest. And so can you.

Take notice

As you get into your bed this evening, think of the comfort it provides and imagine a greater comfort that goes beyond your human imagination—one in which all the struggles of this world fade away. Thank Jesus for being your greatest comfort.

Prayer

Dear Jesus, thank you for being my Savior—for taking my burdens and carrying me through life's trials. Remind me to give my worries over to you, my greatest comfort, and give me the rest you promise. Amen.

week three:

Out and About

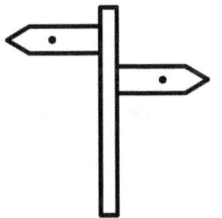

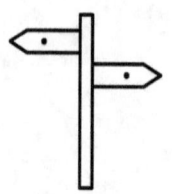

monday

Coffee shop

When you search for me, you will find me; if you seek me with all your heart. Jeremiah 29:13

It was a bright, crisp Sunday morning. My husband and I were dropping our daughter off in a suburb of Chicago so she could catch a ride back to college after spring break. The city was waiting for spring and its promise of new life, but there was no sign of it yet. In fact, there was a dusting of snow on the cars.

As we arrived on the northeast side, I remembered the area from the previous fall, when we had attended a friend's wedding. There was a torrential downpour between the wedding and reception and we ducked into a coffee shop. In addition to shelter from the rain, I enjoyed one of the best lattes I'd ever tasted.

I could picture the cute little coffee shop in my mind, but I couldn't remember the name of it or the exact location. I could almost taste that specialty drink, with its spiced chocolate flavor under a swirly foam top, and I desperately craved another cup.

We began searching and narrowed our target down to a three-block radius near the church where the wedding had been. We Yelped and Googled "coffee shops near me," and came up with about 20. Who knew this random corner of Chicago could have so many?

At one point, we thought we might have found it...the name, *Ipsento*, sounded familiar. But as we approached the building and searched our memories, we both agreed it didn't look right. Disappointed, we drove on.

We finally gave up and settled for another coffee shop. There were only two espresso drink choices. I opted for the Nutella latte, and had to request a ceramic mug rather than the to-go cup the barista was going to serve my drink in. When it finally arrived, the mug was covered with what appeared to be baked on cheese. The barista apologized and remade my drink.

As I finished the last sip of the mediocre coffee, I looked down and saw all the chocolatey Nutella settled at the bottom of the cup. Walking back to the car, the only taste left in my mouth was that of disappointment.

We later discovered that *Ipsento*, the original shop we drove by, *was* that amazing coffee shop! Funny (not funny) how things look completely different in the sunshine when approaching from the opposite direction.

That day's events reminded me that what we really want is often right in front of our eyes. It just doesn't look like we expected. Turns out, the name "Ipsento" comes from the Latin words meaning "self" and "to discover."

On our Lenten journey, we are hoping to discover Jesus, and in so doing, we might also learn some things about ourselves. We'll remember that the grace he offers will fulfill all of our needs, and other substitutes won't satisfy our cravings. The good news is, we don't have to search too hard to find him. He's everywhere–in the everyday, ordinary things that surround us. But if we don't pay attention, we just might miss him.

(To Be Continued…)

Take notice

As we've been doing, take notice of the ordinary things around you. How can your surroundings, like a coffee shop or the perfect latte, remind you of Jesus and his love for you?

Prayer

Jesus, I am searching for you. Show yourself to me in the ordinary, everydayness of my life. Amen.

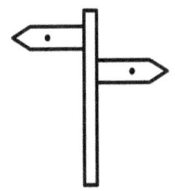

tuesday

Church visits

His father said, "Son, you don't understand. You're with me all the time, and everything that is mine is yours—but this is a wonderful time, and we had to celebrate. This brother of yours was dead, and he's alive! He was lost, and he's found."
Luke 15: 31-32 (MSG)

(Continued from "Coffee Shop")
After locating a coffee shop that wasn't *the* coffee shop, we began looking for a church to attend. It was Sunday morning after all, and even though we were away from home, our usual Sunday morning routine is to worship. Besides, visiting other churches can bring surprises and ideas we can bring back to our own church.

After some Google searching, we decided on Grace Chicago Church, on the city's north side. Our GPS took us right to the school building in which the church met, and we parked easily with information we found on their website. Knowing *where we were going* and *what we were looking for* made all the difference in finding what we wanted.

As we walked into the school building, ladies serving refreshments–grapes, crackers, cheese, and coffee cake–greeted us. People were milling around and talking even though it seemed this was the time the service was supposed to start. We found our way to the auditorium and took our seats.

With an American flag on the wall and storage closets with little-kid-sized chairs stacked on top, the space was much different than our home church. Even though it didn't look like a typical church, after the service, we both agreed it was a pretty phenomenal group of people who provided Christian worship that touched our hearts.

The style was comfortingly familiar, with liturgy, well-known hymns, and a Gospel message straight from the Bible. At the same time, it was refreshingly different with several new-to-us songs and a unique style of communion.

As we drove away, I reflected on our difficulty in finding that coffee shop compared with the ease in finding the church, and I thought, *there must be a lesson in this. Maybe it's that when you're looking for God, you can always find Him.*

But then I thought back to the point the pastor had made in his sermon. He spoke on the parable of the two lost sons, the prodigal son and his older brother (Luke 15:11-32). He explained that the star of the story is the father, who offers unconditional love to both sons. Despite the younger son's turning away and the older son's jealousy, the father was right there (and always had been), ready to lavish his love on them.

On this Lenten journey, we are continually reminded that our salvation is less about our finding God and more about letting God find us. He's reminding us of his presence through our kitchen faucets, our eyeglasses, coffee shops, and more. We aren't *finding him* as much as *he's showing up for us* in our ordinary lives.

If we just open the eyes of our hearts, we will see he's been there all along, waiting to lavish his love on us.

Take notice

If you pass by or attend a service at a house of worship this week, open up your heart and let God find you.

Prayer

God, you are my loving father. I am ready and willing to receive your love. Amen.

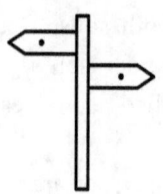

wednesday

lunch at Costco

Jesus said to them, "I am the bread of life. Whoever comes to me will never be hungry, and whoever believes in me will never be thirsty." John 6:35

I should know better than to save my grocery shopping until Saturday. It takes 14 times longer than usual as I search for a parking space, dodge other shoppers and their children with my cart, and stand in long lines. In fact, one of the worst places to shop on a Saturday is Costco.

On one particular Saturday, I entered the store with three things on my list: frozen chicken breasts, romaine lettuce, and blueberries. I left with six things, which I consider a success. I've done worse.

They say don't shop when you're hungry. However, Costco has solved this problem by offering free food samples at the end of every aisle. It's just what a shopper needs to get through a harrowing Saturday shopping trip. Well, sort of.

While I think these little morsels will satisfy my hunger, they really don't. Yes, they satisfy my physical hunger, but there is so much more to a meal than filling my stomach. Little plastic containers and forks, muffin papers, and mini Styrofoam coffee cups do not satisfy my desire for stoneware, glass, and silver. Standing in line waiting for my bite, like a dog waiting for his dish to be filled, won't bring the satisfaction of creating and preparing my own food. Eating beside my grocery cart can't fulfill my need for the comfort I find in our home, sitting in a chair at my kitchen table.

And little bites of oriental chicken and rice, multi-grain chips, cooked salmon, cherry yogurt, apple and gouda smoked sausage, a 2" x 2" square of pizza, topped off with one chocolate-covered almond, do not satisfy my desire for a well-balanced, delicious meal.

In addition, I'm alone. As I rush from one errand to the next, I realize this is just something I have to do, but it's not what I long for. I hunger and thirst for more than calories in a warehouse store.

Our culture attempts to satisfy our longings with short-lived pleasures and earthly desires–a new outfit, jewelry, tech toy, or car. While these may bring momentary happiness, our hearts long for something more substantial.

Unlike samples at Costco, we need a meal like our Lord shared with his disciples on the night he was given over to the guards. A meal with friends, with the family of God. One that, although it is small, satisfies the deep longings of our hearts.

The bread and the wine. The body broken, and the blood poured.

With the feast our Lord provides, we receive the fullness of our hearts' desires. His sacrifice completes us, his goodness comforts us, and his love surrounds us.

Our hearts are satisfied once again.

Take notice

As you shop for groceries and gather for meals this week, consider the life-sustaining meal offered by Jesus. If you have never taken the bread and the cup, find a church or friend who can bring you to the table.

Prayer

Lord, only you can satisfy our deepest hunger and quench our overwhelming thirst. Your love and grace are all we need. Amen.

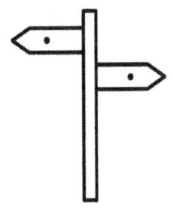

thursday

the Bank

May the Lord make your love increase and overflow for each
other and for everyone else, just as ours does for you.
1 Thessalonians 3:12 (NIV)

I didn't have a piggy bank when I was a kid. But I did have
a bank. I remember it in my mind's eye as a clear cylinder,
about six inches tall and three inches in diameter. Shaped like
a small lantern, it had a green bottom and top, and a stamped-
on business logo I've long since forgotten. In it, I collected
my coins and occasional bills, saving up for something
special.

Before leaving for our vacation at the lake, I'd dig the key
out of my nightstand drawer and unlock my bank. I'd empty

it out into the pockets of my suitcase, so I could have enough for candy at the snack bar and little trinkets from the Five-and-Dime in town.

I was sad to see my empty bank when I came home. With no reserves, it was time to start saving all over again. I knew I couldn't take anything out if I didn't first put something in.

The same holds true today. My "bank" is now a brick-and-mortar building, and the key to my money is my account number and identification. I make deposits. Some are direct, from our places of work. Others involve endorsing a check and slipping it into that clear cylinder and then magically shooting it through its special vacuum-activated tunnel to the teller at the window. Even more magical is that now I can simply take a photo of my check and send it from my cell phone to the bank.

As we make our deposits, our bank accounts fill up. As we withdraw money to pay the bills, it empties. It's really not much different from when I was a kid. I still feel sad (and nervous) when my bank account is low or nearly empty.

Imagine our souls as a bank that takes deposits. When we read God's Word, our souls begin to fill. As we pray and attend worship or Bible study, the balance in our spiritual account rises in turn. The Holy Spirit then fills our hearts even more with the treasure of God's love.

With a full "soul account," we are better able to face struggles and temptations in our day-to-day lives. We have enough reserves to make it through the demands the world places on us. When we have sufficient funds, we can even share with others and give our time and resources to those in need.

Still, if we make too many withdrawals and fail to make deposits, we experience emptiness in our souls that brings us down. As a result, we may focus only on ourselves, fall into temptation, and neglect or lash out at others.

When our spiritual balance is low, it's time to replenish our reserves once again. God calls us to dwell in his Word, to reach out to him in prayer, and to open our hearts in praise and worship. When we earnestly seek him, the Holy Spirit will fill us, and God's love can once again overflow.

Take notice

As you write a check, make a deposit, or pass by a bank this week, think of ways to fill your spiritual bank account.

Prayer

Lord, fill me up with your love so that I might have more than enough to share with others. Amen.

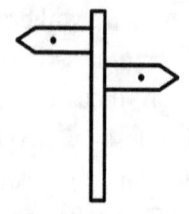

friday

Shoe store

*Beloved, since God loved us so much, we also ought to love
one another. No one has ever seen God; if we love one
another, God abides in us, and his love is perfected in us.*
1 John 4:11-12

I walked into Discount Shoe Warehouse (a.k.a. DSW)
needing a new pair of shoes.

I like DSW because of the vast selection. Tennis shoes,
casual shoes, dress shoes. Short boots, tall boots, slippers.
Flats, heels, and platforms. Leather, suede, and canvas. Blue,
black, brown, white, and every other color in the rainbow.

I found the shoes I wanted and went to wait in line to
make my purchase.

That's when I noticed the people. Like the shoes on the shelves, a diverse group surrounded me. Shoppers and workers. Bodies of different shapes, sizes, and colors. Behind me stood two women in traditional Amish or Mennonite clothing. They were speaking to each other in German. Then a family walked in the door speaking Spanish.

As I watched and listened to the surrounding people, I made assumptions—maybe even judgments—about their lives, their status, or their beliefs. I know it's a natural human tendency to look at someone and make an assumption or judgment based on a first impression. But how often are those assumptions proven wrong when we get to know someone—really know them?

I looked again at the shoes. And I thought about the people. I imagined walking in their shoes.

Have you ever wondered how it would feel to walk in someone else's shoes for a day? If we could experience the life of other human beings, what would we learn about them? And what would we learn about ourselves?

Each person we encounter has a whole life attached to them that we cannot see at first glance. Each one carries pain and sadness, worry and stress. Hopefully, they also carry love and joy, and some happiness. But how can we know? We can't walk in their shoes.

Our world is full of diversity. And as for people, Jesus told us how to handle our differences. It's really not complicated.

Jesus commanded us to, "*love one another. Just as I have loved you, you also should love one another.*" (John 13:34b) He didn't say to love only the people you know. Or to love the people just like yourself. He even called us to love our enemies. We are to love one another. Period.

We can start loving one another by saying "hello," being kind to strangers, and refraining from making assumptions based on outward appearances. Having conversations that focus on listening can go a long way toward understanding. Offering a helping hand or being willing to take one yourself are great ways to show and experience love.

Take notice

Look at the shoes you and others are wearing today. Imagine spending a day in another's shoes or them spending a day in yours.

Prayer

Lord, let me show others the love you have given me. Help my words and actions to be deserving of the love you give so freely. Amen.

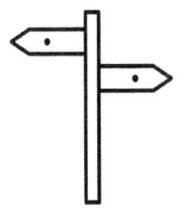

saturday

the Library

Thanks be to God for his indescribable gift!
2 Corinthians 9:15

I love a good bookstore. Whether it's a big Barnes and Noble with its own Starbucks or a small independent bookseller in an old house with that dusty book smell, I'm drawn in as I glance over the reading selection or browse the best-seller table. The richness and variety, the wealth of words, and depths of knowledge and imagination are vast.

And while it's fun to browse, I can't know what lies between the covers unless I read the book. That recently released novel sparks my interest, and I turn it over to find the price: $25.99. Ouch. I can pay less at the bargain book display, but they're still not free. There are costs to produce the book and writers have to eat. (Thanks for buying this book and paying for this writer's supper!)

I've bought many books over the years. The brimming bookshelves in my home and boxes full of books I've donated prove it. That being said, my pocketbook and my shelves have limits. Buying every book I want to read isn't feasible. Thankfully, there is the library.

My husband works at a library. My daughter is going to school to become a librarian. Over time, they have sold me on the benefits of libraries. Our public libraries offer a wide selection of books, old and new. They offer cooking and crafting classes, children's story hour, and book clubs. They provide internet access and quiet, cozy corners for reading, writing, or studying.

But the best part? They do all of this for free! Typically, the only price you pay is the time it takes to apply for a library card. Give them your name and address, show a photo ID, and you're in! It's all yours for the asking.

It's the same way with God's grace. How often do we feel we need to earn our salvation? We think going to church, doing good works, and avoiding all temptation and sin will earn us the promises in God's Word. We want the assurance that God loves us unconditionally and forgives our sins. How could something so wonderful be free?

God's Word says it is. Like signing up for your library card, you only have to ask for grace. It's free for the taking. God loves us so much that he generously gives us this freebie until we can't help but return to him with thanks.

When we buy or borrow a book, the whole point is to read it. In doing so, we fulfill our curiosity and desire for knowledge or entertainment. In the same way, when we receive grace, we fulfill our purpose to live as God's children by worshiping him, serving others, and attempting to live a right and faithful life. Those "works" are not the cost of grace. They are a grateful response to it.

Take notice

The next time you pass by a library, remember the free gift of God's grace. If you can, stop in and check out a book or sign up for a library card–it's free!

Prayer

Oh God, thank you for the marvelous gift of grace that costs me nothing. Help me show my gratitude through a life of faithfulness, worship, and service. Amen.

week four:

Nature Walk

monday

F.o.m.o.

For I am not ashamed of the gospel; it is God's saving power for everyone who believes, for the Jew first and also for the Greek. Romans 1:16

I confess I'm a slave to social media. Scrolling through, I see what my friends are up to, where they've traveled, and what they or their kids have accomplished. I try to avoid the FOMO feeling and instead celebrate the joys and adventures of others without that "fear of missing out." I'll admit, it's not always easy, and sometimes I do fall into the FOMO trap, wishing *their* story was *my* story.

On the flip side, I frequently share photos of *my* life, *my* family, and *my* adventures. But do my selfies and pictures cause a FOMO for my friends? Finding the balance between keeping everything to myself and sharing too much is a challenge.

Taking photos to capture my memories is another downfall of mine. I often go overboard, snapping shot after shot, and regret it afterward, realizing I was so intent on taking pictures that I missed out on the moment.

Thankfully, God has given me reminders to put the phone down, ponder, and connect with him and others.

One of those reminders came during a bike ride on a spring afternoon. A pack of baby minks scuttled across the road in front of me. I stopped as quickly as I could and fumbled with my phone to capture the incredible moment. But they moved too fast for me. I knew if I looked at my phone long enough to turn the camera on, focus it, and snap the picture, I would miss the entire experience myself.

So I stopped and put my camera down. I captured their cute furry black bodies, their beady, bright eyes, and their squeaky, incessant chatter in my mind's eye and recorded it all somewhere in my memory bank. I was amazed and grateful for this wonder of God's creation that He had placed in my path.

I may not have had any pictures to share, but afterward I shared my story with many friends and family (and now on this page with even more people). Whether in photos or in words, when we have a good story to share, it's hard to keep it to ourselves!

I began writing several years ago, never intending for it to go beyond my family and friends. But God had other ideas in mind. He gave me moments that turned into stories he wanted me to share. Stories of love and forgiveness. Of blessings received and taken away. Of mercy and grace.

He's given me another story that I can't help sharing. It's a story that no one needs to have a "fear of missing out" on. This story is for me and for you. It's the story of the One who gave his life so that we might live.

As we continue on our Lenten journey, I hope you find the story of unconditional love on the path in front of you. There's no need to miss out. It can be your story too!

🔍 Take notice

The next time you get ready to snap a photo with your camera, put it down, and thank God for blessing you with the moment instead.

🙏 Prayer

God, you have given me an amazing story of unconditional love. Help me to make that story my story. Amen.

tuesday

Evergreens

Look, I will tell you a mystery! We will not all die, but we will all be changed, in a moment, in the twinkling of an eye, at the last trumpet. For the trumpet will sound, and the dead will be raised imperishable, and we will be changed.
1 Corinthians 15:51-52

Having grown up as the daughter of a Christmas tree grower, I can't help but be fond of evergreen trees. While the deciduous maples, oaks, elms, and birch trees lose their leaves and appear as dead lifeless branches throughout the winter, the evergreen stays, well, ever green.

Imagine how different the landscape in our northern climates would appear if there was no green throughout the winter months. Watching the monochromatic gray and black tree branches and trunks sway against the white snow would be like watching TV back in the 1960s.

Instead, life is in technicolor. And thanks to the evergreens, walks outside during the cold winter and early days of spring are colorful as well. The lush green reminds us of life. It also reminds us that spring is coming.

During the early days of Lent, the world around us seems lifeless. Crocuses have yet to peek through the soil. Daffodils are finishing their sleep underground as well. The trees lie dormant.

But even when the world appears dead, life is forming. In the darkness below the ground, seeds have germinated and are bursting with shoots reaching up through the dirt toward the sun. Tree branches hold buds that will turn into leaves of every shape and color. Birds are laying eggs, soon to become hatchlings, and wild animals also carry the bulging signs of new life.

On Ash Wednesday, we were reminded that "dust we are, and to dust we shall return." Before we had life breathed into us, we were as lifeless as dried-up seeds or withered plants. And in the blink of an eye, our bodies could be lifeless again.

While the plants around us sleep, it's easy to assume there is no life in them.

But look! It's an evergreen tree! It's also sleeping for the winter, but it sleeps with the color of life cloaking its branches. And it's pointing up to the sky. Look up!

In just a few weeks, we will lift our eyes to the cross–the cross on which our Savior died. His sacrifice bears our sins and his death brings the promise of everlasting, bursting-like-spring life.

🔍 *Take notice*

Notice the evergreen trees around you. Remember the gift of life that is yours both here and now and in God's eternal kingdom.

🙏 *Prayer*

Lord, Thank you for the gift of eternal life that is ours through your sacrifice and immeasurable grace. Amen.

wednesday

Trees in the wind

For you shall go out in joy
and be led forth in peace;
the mountains and the hills before you
shall break forth into singing,
and all the trees of the field shall clap their hands.
Isaiah 55:12 (ESV)

Sturdy oak and maple trees, reaching 60 or 70 feet, surround our home in southwest Michigan. When the wind blows, the leaves rustle and the robust trunks sway. This bending and swaying have a strengthening effect on the trees, as it helps their roots grow deeper.

But I remember a late winter windstorm that was not so gentle. Sustained straight-line winds at 55-60 miles per hour brought a continuous blast that sounded like a freight train hurtling through our backyard. The trees tossed and turned wildly. Still, as far as I could tell, not one broke.

During a different season, this wind may have brought down some of those staunch oaks and resolute maples. They would have snapped or been uprooted, unable to withstand such a penetrating force.

So why not this time? And by the same token, why do some challenges in life rock our faith and break us, while others make our faith grow stronger?

Like the trees, we are blown by the winds of life. Through difficulties and doubts, the Holy Spirit, like a gentle wind, nudges us to move and bend. We lean into questions that can strengthen our beliefs, and we grow into our understanding just as a tree's bark slowly expands around its ever-widening girth.

But how can we withstand the gale-force winds that life can bring us? The trees in my backyard might show us the way.

First, in late winter, those trees were bare and had nothing for the wind to grasp onto. It might have been different if they'd been weighed down with summer leaves or winter snow and ice. In the same way, if we hang on to the weight of this world–the tragedies we see on the news, our possessions, our success, our worries–too tightly, we're more likely to break under the weight of our burdens when life's strong winds blow.

Second, the trees in my backyard must have been healthy. If they had been filled with rot or insect damage, they would have snapped in those winds. Like the trees, if we allow sin to eat away at our souls and infest our lives, difficult life events may rock our faith. Instead, God calls us to confess those sins, and he will forgive them.

Finally, those trees had deep roots. Likewise, when our faith-roots run deep–strengthened through worship, prayer, Bible reading, and fellowship with other believers–they will keep us strong and remind us to turn to God during times of difficulty.

Like the towering oaks and sturdy maples, let's reach toward heaven in praise of the One who gives us life and sustains us through life's storms!

 Take notice

Notice the trees near you today, and remember what makes them strong. Then remember a stormy time in your life and recall if your faith faltered or sustained you.

Prayer

Dear Lord, help the roots of my faith to grow deep, remove the weight of this world from me, and wipe away the rot of sin from my heart so my faith will stay strong in the face of difficulties. Amen.

thursday

Equinox

For everything there is a season and a time for every matter under heaven. Ecclesiastes 3:1

The days are getting longer. Light filtering through my bedroom curtains awakens me in the morning. And afternoons stretch into evenings as the sun lingers a few minutes more with each passing day.

The winter solstice, the longest night of the year, with its dark shadows and reminders of grief, is behind us now. The longest day, our summer solstice, awaits us with the promise of long evening walks and bike rides, and late sunsets at the beach.

But along our Lenten journey we will come to the middle. The spring equinox, near the end of March, is one of two days on the calendar when the hours of darkness are equal to the hours of light. It's the halfway point, in which there's a balance of light and darkness for a moment in time. The equinoxes (in spring and fall), from the Latin words meaning "equal night," are the only two days of the year when there are 12 hours of light and 12 hours of darkness everywhere on the Earth.

While these facts not only point to our great Creator God, who fashioned an amazing universe, they also give us a framework through which to view our lives.

While daylight helps many plants and animals grow and prosper, darkness offers an equally important time to rest. Work and rest, growth and reflection, joy and sadness–there is *a time for every purpose under heaven.* (Ec. 3:1b, KJV)

The equinox reminds us of the balance we should strive for in our own lives. God asks us to find balance, letting nothing overtake us like the deep nights of winter or the lingering days of summer. Instead, we should aim to bring calm to the chaos and harmony to the discord.

It strikes me that the equinox is not only equal hours of day and night; it's also equal around the globe, save for the fact that when it's night in the east, it's day in the west, and vice versa. Perhaps our Creator God is reminding us of the equality he gave to all; the harmony he had intended for his whole creation.

But our world is sinful and broken. There is not one place or person living or dead that hasn't entered darkness. As followers of Christ, we are called to be peacemakers and justice-seekers, to bring Christ's light into our fallen world.

As Jesus prayed—*Your kingdom come, your will be done, on earth as it is in heaven*—so God longs for all people to experience the tranquility he originally created. Through Christ's death and resurrection we have the promise that he *will* make all things right.

Thanks be to God that the darkness that is here for a time will be overcome by the light of his son, Jesus Christ.

Take notice

Note the day of the spring equinox on your calendar. If possible, watch the sunrise or sunset (or both!) on that day and thank God for his marvelous creation.

Prayer

Lord of the universe, your wonders never cease. Be with me in the darkness as in the light. Bring balance to my life and help me bring peace and harmony to your world. Through Jesus, your son. Amen.

friday

Roadside litter and crocuses

*If we confess our sins, he who is faithful and just will forgive
us our sins and cleanse us from all unrighteousness.*
1 John 1:9

It was a gray day in the middle of Lent but warm enough for
me to set out on a bike ride. Not long into my ride, something
red in the roadside brush caught my eye. Could it be a robin,
the first sign of spring? I slowed my bicycle and looked
closer, only to find...a red Solo cup, carelessly tossed aside.

As I rode along, the dirt that had been covered up for
months with winter snow, was now revealed. The closer I
looked, the more trash I noticed. Fast food cups, plastic
power drink bottles, and newspapers suffocating in blue

72

plastic bags. Previously hidden by a blanket of snow, it was now there for everyone to see.

I continued to ride, surveying the crimes of human nature against Mother Nature. A big orange bouncy ball, separated from its child. A snow brush, lost from its car. An old mattress, tattered, stained, and shameful, lying naked with no coverlet.

The trash reminded me of my sin, which might be easy to hide for a while but is eventually uncovered. Selfishness, pride, gossip, greed, laziness, and a host of other failings came to mind. What else had I covered up? Lying? Cheating? Jealousy? Looking down on others? My instinct was to hide my sin and avoid my shame.

But this is the season of Lent. A time for examining, confessing, and repenting.

The snow has melted; the cover-up is gone. Now is the time to look at the litter. To clean it up. To pluck it from the brambles of our souls.

But how do we begin this process of "spring cleaning" our lives? God calls us to examine our actions and the motivations behind them. If we are honest, we will find intentions that put ourselves and our desires before his. If we pour out our weaknesses to him humbly and sincerely, he will listen. God's forgiveness will wash us clean, and we'll need no further cover-up.

Once we've confessed to God, we are free to confess to a trusted friend, spouse, counselor, or pastor. In being vulnerable with others, we're more likely to make the changes God desires in us. By asking for forgiveness, we also begin the healing process that will allow our relationships to grow and flourish.

As I continued my ride, I again noticed a bright color in the roadside brush. This time, something purple. Another ball? A hat or glove? When it came into focus, I smiled.

There in the dead, dry grasses and leaves, a small patch of crocuses had thrust themselves through the muck. With petals outstretched like hands in worship, they seemed to celebrate the renewal that was coming. They promised hope on this overcast mid-Lenten day.

🔍 Take notice

Take a walk or slow ride today and search for roadside litter. (You could even bring a trash bag and pick it up!) Then confess your sins to God and ask him to forgive.

🙏 Prayer

Dear God, I confess to you today the sins of my heart. Wash me clean with your son's precious blood, and renew my spirit so that I may walk in your ways. Amen.

saturday

Dogwoods

But thanks be to God, who gives us the victory through our Lord Jesus Christ. 1 Corinthians 15:57

My husband and I spent our April honeymoon in Tennessee. As we drove down from the northwest corner of Indiana and made our way toward Gatlinburg and the Smoky Mountains, we watched as the trees changed from brown to green and the flowers appeared in stunning colors. Best of all were the dogwood trees.

I hadn't really paid much attention to dogwoods before that. But in mid-April Tennessee, one can't ignore them. The dogwoods, along with redbud trees, are in their peak blooming season at that time.

I soon learned to recognize and love the dogwood trees at home as well. Their light petals floating in the air bring a lightness that lifts my spirit.

It wasn't until years later that I learned about the Legend of the Dogwood, a story born out of the early Christians' love for their Lord. Although the tree has a small trunk and twisted branches, according to legend, it was once the strongest tree in the Middle East. So strong that its wood was used to make the cross on which the Roman soldiers crucified Jesus.

The legend tells how upset the tree was that its wood was used for killing. Jesus promised the tree that it would no longer grow tall and strong, so its wood couldn't be used for a cross again.

The dogwood's flowers form the shape of a cross with four petals, two longer and two shorter ones. On the outside edges of the petals are small holes, or indentations, reminiscent of the nail holes in Jesus' hands. These "holes" even have a tinge of red or brown, reminding us of Jesus' shed blood. In the center of the flower is a small green cluster that resembles our Lord's crown of thorns.

The story is a legend, but I am drawn to the creativity of those early Christians and the love they had for their Savior. I'm also drawn to the beauty of the dogwood tree. Every spring, I look forward to seeing it blossom in praise of its maker.

I hope dogwood trees grow in your neck of the woods. If they do, when you see them bloom this spring, remember the cross. Stop and give thanks to our Creator God for the details he masterfully formed in his creation. Then thank him for the gift of his Son. As the petals float gently on the twisted branches, let your heart be lifted, knowing that your sins have been washed away.

Take notice

Look for dogwood trees in bloom or look up pictures of the tree if they don't grow in your area. Notice the shape of the tree and inspect the intricacies of the flowers.

Prayer

Lord, thank you for the beautiful trees of spring and for the promise of new life in You. Amen.

week five:

Infrastructure

monday

to Build below

Everyone, then, who hears these words of mine and acts on them will be like a wise man who built his house on rock.
Matthew 7:24

I rarely think about infrastructure.

The word comes up during political debates or on the news when there is concern over crumbling infrastructure. I picture the big steel and concrete walls and columns that I've seen in Chicago when using the underground parking garages and driving on Lower Lower Wacker Drive. When I hear about failing infrastructure, I picture these columns and walls crumbling under the weight of the city, and everything tumbling down and being swallowed up by Lake Michigan.

Like the city has been sitting on a giant sinkhole all these years, and no one realized it.

The word infrastructure comes from the Latin roots "infra-" meaning "below" and "struere" meaning "to build." It's the foundation on which a city or country is built. It refers to the physical structures, like highways, water and sewer systems, electrical grids, etc. The success or failure of a city, state, or nation's economy often relies on the success or failure of this infrastructure.

Just like our cities, if we build our houses over a sinkhole, they stand the chance of being swallowed up. It reminds me of the song I sang as a kid in Sunday school:

The wise man built his house upon the rock...(repeat twice)
And the rains came tumbling down.
The rains came down and the floods came up...(repeat twice)
And the house on the rock stood firm.

(Demonstrated by our fists in our hands.)

If you know the song, you know what happened to the foolish man's house–the one that was built on the sand. It fell flat! (And we all clapped our hands together.) Even though the foolish man was told he needed a solid infrastructure, he didn't listen.

Jesus told the parable of the wise and foolish builders (Matt. 7:24-27) to bring home the point that those who hear his words and live by them have a solid foundation in their lives. When the trials of life rain down on them, they remain standing on the rock that is their faith. But those who hear Jesus' words and don't follow them would struggle in difficult times.

During this fifth week of Lent, we'll think about the infrastructure that surrounds us; that foundation we often ignore. And yet, without that "building-under," we would have trouble at every turn.

In the same way, without the solid rock of Jesus as the foundation of our faith and our lives, we would find ourselves blown over by the winds and rains–the cares and crises of this broken world in which we live. In thinking of it that way, there's only one thing to do. As little children still sing:

> *So build your life on the Lord Jesus Christ*
> *Build your life on the Lord Jesus Christ,*
> *Build your life on the Lord Jesus Christ,*
> *And the blessings will come down.*

Take notice

Look at the buildings and homes around you and notice their foundations. Think about the foundation of your life.

Prayer

Lord Jesus Christ, I want to build my life on you. Be my solid rock, I pray. Amen.

tuesday

Cracks in the pavement

But he said to me, "My grace is sufficient for you, for power is made perfect in weakness." So I will boast all the more gladly of my weaknesses, so that the power of Christ may dwell in me. 2 Corinthians 12:9

As I walk down our little country road, I see the effects of our cold winter on the pavement. Our freezing temperatures, ice, and snow cause it to contract. Then, as the warmth of spring arrives, it expands. The result? Many cracks have formed in the asphalt. Without traffic, our road may have had a chance, but it crumbles under the weight of heavy cars and trucks.

Year after year, the cracks increase. Our neighborhood pays to have the cracks sealed and the holes patched, but by the next year, more of both have appeared. And then more patches. What once was a smooth untainted surface is now rough and unsightly. And when I drive my car and ride my bike on other nearby roads, I can see that the problem of crumbling roads is widespread.

It occurs to me that these bumpy, patched-up roads resemble our lives. When our hearts freeze up and refuse to let Jesus in, we become hardened to his promises. Eventually, the cracks that emerge from our instability allow sin to enter our lives. We try to cover up the sin, to put a patch over it, but hiding doesn't work. More cracks form right alongside the old. Small wrongs grow into bigger transgressions, and gradually our lives are filled with potholes.

The weight of the world and the burdens we carry–worries, responsibilities, health, and relationships–all add pressure to our already imperfect lives. On our own, we don't stand a chance.

As I continue my walk along our damaged road, I notice little sprouts of grass and flowers emerging through the cracks. These small openings in the blacktop have allowed seeds, rain, and even sunshine to get through. Even in the ugliness of a broken road, life and beauty find a way through.

What a beautiful picture of how Jesus finds his way into our frozen and hardened hearts. Like a seed that falls between the cracks, the Holy Spirit finds our weaknesses and transforms us from the inside out. The rain of forgiveness and the sunshine of Jesus' love bring about the change we need.

We may not be as strong as a smooth, new highway, but in our weakness, he brings forth something alive and beautiful.

Through his grace and forgiveness, we can find new life despite our failings. And beauty is born out of brokenness.

Take notice

Go for a walk and notice the cracks in the road and sidewalks. Remember something good that came from your own weakness.

Prayer

Dear Jesus, bring the warmth of your love into my frozen heart today, and through your grace bring new life and beauty from my shortcomings. Amen.

wednesday

Power lines

Now to him who is able to do immeasurably more than all we ask or imagine, according to his power that is at work within us, to him be glory in the church and in Christ Jesus throughout all generations, for ever and ever! Amen.
Ephesians 3:20-21

Power. We take it for granted. We flip a switch and the light goes on. Our laptop or phone dies, and we charge it up. Toasters, coffeemakers, refrigerators, garage doors. We pay no attention to the power that keeps them going. We take it as a matter of course.

Until the power goes out. We are lost and frustrated without it. *Where are the candles? Do we have any matches? My phone is dead. Well, this is just great!*

When I'm walking in our neighborhood, I pass under huge power lines. Draped from pole to pole, like superheroes with metal arms outstretched, they hold the power to our and our neighbors' homes. Immovable giants, they line up for miles. On a quiet day, you can sometimes hear them buzz.

I don't really understand where the power comes from. I know it takes fossil fuels, wind turbines, or solar panels, and somehow power is born. From there, it mysteriously gets transferred to wires above our heads and comes to my home via more lines buried under the ground.

This mysterious energy that brings us light, whose origins most of us don't understand, is something we all depend on. We can't imagine living without it.

In many ways, the power of God is like electricity. We don't understand the mystery of his infinite origins. His power sent the planets into orbit and lit up the sun. Every morning that sun rises, and in the evening it sets. We depend on it and, in fact, can't live without it.

Then there's the mystery of Jesus' saving power. He has shown us great love in laying down his life! He bled and died for us, and there's power in that blood; power to forgive sins, to conquer death and hell, and to offer us unlimited grace and infinite love.

God's power and the saving power of Jesus' sacrifice are free and reliable. No electric bills, no shut-offs when life gets stormy. No searching around in the dark for a source of light. Our light source–his power–is always on and available.

Let's not take this power for granted but give thanks for it today. Thank God for his creation. Express gratitude for his saving grace. Stand in awe of his power.

Let's turn on the Light, live in it, and let it shine on everyone we meet.

🔍 Take notice

When you use electricity today, remember the power of God's almighty hand and the saving blood of Jesus.

🙏 Prayer

Dear Lord Jesus, thank you for your saving power, given freely to all who believe. I believe, Lord. Shine your light on me. Amen.

thursday

Bridges

*Jesus answered, "I am the way and the truth and the life. No
one comes to the Father except through me. John 14:6*

Can you see the beauty in bridges?

I can't help it. Every time I ride my bike over one, I have
an overwhelming urge to take a picture. I often do. And when
riding shotgun while my husband drives, I've snapped many a
photo as we've approached a bridge.

Maybe it's their symmetry. Metal riveted to metal in
perfect geometric shapes against the backdrop of blue sky. Or
it could be their nostalgia. Old wooden, especially covered,
bridges that are engraved with the signature of the buggies
that once rolled over them.

Mammoth, modern bridges connecting cable upon cable to span a distance that boggles the mind. Wonders of the industrial age, these engineering masterpieces are as beautiful as they are functional.

As we approach a bridge, I am in awe. But as we cross, I look down. If I'm on my bike or walking, I will stop and peer over the side rails. I am captivated by the sights below–usually a river, a stream, or some other body of water. Sometimes, the water is deep and wide. Dangers lurk below its surface. Swirling currents, immovable rocks, and slithering creatures can bring a chill of fear.

Before people built bridges, crossing the water was difficult. Their options were to swim, paddle, or ride their swimming horses across. It was treacherous, and some even lost their lives trying to cross over. Without a way to the other side, a person was trapped and disconnected from hopes, dreams, or family on the opposite bank.

During this season of Lent, as we reflect on our human failings and sins, we're also feeling disconnected–from God. There is a vast distance between the shore we stand on–the world that holds a tight grip on us–and the heavenly kingdom we yearn to be a part of. We long for peace and the embrace of our heavenly Father.

Were we to attempt crossing that ocean of wrongs on our own strength, we would surely drown. We could hop in a boat and try to row across, but the currents are strong and the distance is long. We need a bridge.

The bridge we long for is shaped like an old rugged cross. Jesus laid down his life on it so that we could cross safely over that great divide.

What an incredible bridge! What a remarkable gift!

Take notice

The next time you cross a bridge, thank Jesus for laying down his life to bridge the divide between you and your heavenly Father.

Prayer

Dear Jesus, we praise you for allowing us to cross freely over the waters of death to the shores of life. Amen.

friday

Streetlights

Your word is a lamp to my feet and a light to my path.
Psalm 119:105

Walk along any city sidewalk or drive any suburban street
and you'll notice the streetlights. Or, as often happens, you
may not notice them. Streetlights are the type of thing we
don't notice when they're there and working. But when they
go out, we can get lost in their absence.

As the sun sets, the solar sensors know that it's time to
turn on the lights. Glowing at first, and then fluorescent
white, the lights shine on our way. Where one light leaves off,
the next one begins, so we're never in the dark. We can
clearly see the way ahead.

I grew up on a farm. Out in the middle of the country, there are no streetlights. Still, we had a yard light. A big, bright beacon in the middle of the driveway and yard. We could easily run outside after dark to tell Dad supper was almost ready. It never seemed scary as long as we were in the light.

I've tried to walk paths and sidewalks in the dark. I find it frightening. Will I step into a hole and twist my ankle? Or trip over debris? Or will some wild creature emerge from the shadows and overtake me without warning?

Life is like those dark alleys and paths. When we don't have a clear sense of direction, we can lose our way and stray from the way God intends for us. We feel lost and confused when unfortunate events or circumstances–an illness, loss of a job, or a broken relationship–throw us off course. When we aren't able to see the "right path" we open ourselves up to the forces of sin. As we walk dark paths in fear, the sins of addiction, greed, selfishness, or lust can easily overtake us.

We need to find a light–a beacon to show us the way home. We need to open God's word and let it guide our footsteps, our words, and our actions.

By your words I can see where I'm going;
they throw a beam of light on my dark path.
(Ps. 119:105, MSG)

Taking a few minutes each day to listen to or read God's word will help us find our way through a world that seems dark and on a journey that is filled with trouble. His word is our streetlight.

🔍 Take notice

Put the Holy Bible app on your phone. When you see a streetlight or wish there was one, open that app and read a few verses from God's word.

🙏 Prayer

Heavenly Father, let your word light my path. Help me to follow the way you have shown me. Amen.

saturday

Airports

If we confess our sins, he who is faithful and just will forgive
us our sins and cleanse us from all unrighteousness.
1 John 1:9

Airports. No one really likes them, do they?

During the four years our daughter attended school in Minnesota, we often had to pick her up at Midway, the smaller airport in Chicago. It was under construction for over a year, and on one particular night it was an especially loud nuisance. As we pulled up in the bumper-to-bumper "Arrivals" traffic, the sound of jackhammers and loud metal banging against metal reverberated off the concrete pillars that surrounded us.

When my husband opened the door to load the bags, the noise crescendoed to a level that startled me.

"I hate airports!" my daughter complained as she climbed into the back seat.

"I hear ya! This place is crazy!" I turned around and feasted my eyes on my baby girl. It had been a couple of months since I had seen her.

"Hi, honey. You're almost home!"

"Thank goodness!" She plopped down next to our little dog who had been anxiously awaiting her arrival. Cuddles all around. We merged out into the traffic, our GPS guiding us home.

Even though we may not appreciate the airports and the tiny airplane seats, we want what they can deliver to us. Or the places they can deliver us to. Planes bring our children home to us, and fly us out to visit friends or family. They allow us to travel across the country in only a few hours and bring us to other parts of the world that, without airplanes and airports, would take weeks to reach.

On our journey to the cross during Lent, we may encounter some uncomfortable situations.

Let's start with confession. We don't like to go there. It's difficult to admit our sins, both the wrongs we've done and the good we've left undone.

Next comes repentance. It's one thing to admit our wrongs, but it's another to turn away from our behavior, commit to better ways, and make restitution to those we've hurt. To approach the friend, child, spouse, or parent that we have wronged and honestly admit our weakness is awkward and humbling. To bring the remorse for our sins to our God in prayer can leave us feeling naked and embarrassed.

Once our burden is lifted, and we have received the forgiveness we need, we open our eyes and see that we have arrived. The journey has brought us home to where we belong. We're in our Savior's loving arms once again.

When we are right with God, the trip through confession and repentance is so worth it. Won't you come home today?

Take notice

When you see a plane in the sky today, think of areas of your life that make you uncomfortable in your walk with the Lord, and what's needed to get you to a better place.

Prayer

Lord, I confess that I have done things I shouldn't, and have left undone those things I should have done. Forgive me, Lord, and welcome me back into your loving arms again. Amen.

week six:

People

monday

what's in a Name?

He calls his own sheep by name and leads them out.
John 10:3b

Have you ever had one of those embarrassing moments when you call a friend by the wrong name?

It happened to me twice in two days. I called Rachel "Gwen." I had confused a young, tall and slender graduate student who had interned with me with another young, tall and slender graduate student who also had interned with me. Still, I was Facebook friends with both of them, we had kept in touch, and there was no reason for me to have gotten the name wrong.

The other friend, Lisa, I called "Melissa." Here, I mixed up a physical therapist coworker from a previous job with another PT I had once worked with. When Lisa returned to my current world of work, I could not remember which PT from my past life she was.

I blame it on my age. But I know that, really, I have never been too good with names. In order to remember a name, I either must know a person well and have spent a lot of time with them, or I create a mnemonic device from the get-go.

If I don't do one of those two things, I will embarrass myself from time to time. I apologize, hopefully, before they correct me or think I don't care about them enough to remember their name.

And that's really the bottom line, isn't it? When we learn someone's name, it shows we care about them. We go that extra mile to make them feel special. My kids' favorite teachers were those who not only knew their names but took the time to come up with special nicknames for them that brought out one of their positive characteristics. Their least favorite teachers were those that didn't bother to learn their names. Like the band director who pointed to my neighbor girl in her senior year of band, after eight years as her director, and said, "You!"

When someone knows our name or calls us by our name, we know we mean something to them.

That's why it's so comforting to know that Jesus knows my name. He, the Son of God, knows *MY* name. He also knows *YOUR* name. When he told the parable of the lost sheep, Jesus, the Good Shepherd, showed us how well he knows us:

The gatekeeper opens the gate to him and the sheep recognize his voice. He calls his own sheep by name and leads them out....I am the Good Shepherd. I know my own sheep and my own sheep know me. In the same way, the Father knows me and I know the Father. I put the sheep before myself, sacrificing myself if necessary. (John 10: 3, 14-15, MSG)

He knows my story. He knows my heart. Jesus knows my name.

🔍 Take notice

Remember the words of the Good Shepherd when someone says or writes your name today.

🙏 Prayer

Good Shepherd, thank you for knowing and remembering my name. Help me to hear your voice when you call me. Amen.

tuesday

Contacts

For "everyone who calls on the name of the Lord shall be saved." Romans 10:13

When I was a kid, I had a cute little address book. I think it was black and white with a red cat on it, but it's been gone so long that I can't say for sure.

With pencil and eraser marks, it was filled with all of my closest friends' names, addresses, and home phone numbers. There were no cell phones back then, so their phone number connected with their family's home phone, and everyone in their family. When you dialed their number, you might get their mom, dad, sister, or brother.

If you wanted to invite your friend to a party or send them a message, you found their address, wrote it on the envelope, inserted your message, licked it shut, and slapped on a stamp (which you also had to lick first). A few days later, they would receive your message or invitation.

My, how times have changed!

My address book is now "my contacts," and I carry it with me at all times. My call will go straight to that person, whether they are at home, at work, or on vacation. Their phone will light up with my number, my name, and maybe even my picture. If they want to talk to me, they'll pick up. And if they're busy, I'll leave them a message.

Or I could just start with a message. Through texting, email, Facebook message, or Snapchat, I can invite them to meet me for coffee or get my message to them as quickly as I can type it. I can send them a photo to show them what I'm thinking about or doing. And within seconds, I often get a response.

We've come a long way since the paper address books, telephones mounted on the wall, and snail-mail of the past. Although our connections with others have changed, there's one contact that has never changed.

My connection with my God is the same today as it was for our ancestors centuries ago. When we need Him, we call on Him and He is there. He listens to our every thought and prayer. No dialing, no writing, no typing. He has made it so easy to call on him. I wonder why we don't do so more often.

God is waiting for our call. He's not standing by or staring at his phone. He's standing right by our side and keeping his watchful eye on us. Always ready for us to pour out the message of our hearts to him. And if we take time to listen, we will hear his voice.

Take notice

When you use your contacts or your phone today, take a moment to contact God first. Share the message on your heart, and listen for his voice.

Prayer

Dear God, help me remember you want to hear from me. And thank you for always picking up when I call. Amen.

wednesday

Growing up

But the fruit of the Spirit is love, joy, peace, forbearance, kindness, goodness, faithfulness. Galatians 5:22

Our perceptions of growth depend on our vantage point. Sometimes change is surprising and extraordinary. At other times, it's hidden and imperceptible.

Take, for example, the growth of a child. When we run into friends we haven't seen in a while, it strikes us how much their kids have grown. By comparison, our own kids seem to grow slowly. We mark their heights with pencil on the doorframes so we can prove they have grown. Those pencil marks, as well as their increasing shoe sizes, are the outward signs that confirm they are growing.

Over the years, I know I've grown spiritually. You probably have as well. But can others perceive it? If we can't measure our spiritual growth with a ruler, are there other ways to show we've grown?

Spiritual practices, such as praying, reading the Bible, meditating, fasting, confessing, and simplifying, are wonderful ways of becoming closer to God. They will strengthen our faith and make us more resilient in the face of temptation. But these practices and perceptions are only evident to ourselves, or perhaps those very close to us. Like a pearl growing from a grain of sand inside a clam's shell, beautiful things are happening inside, though that change is not visible on the outside.

There are several indicators that alert those around us of the transformation that is happening in our hearts and minds. These practices bring our inner beauty in Christ to the surface.

Through **loving others unconditionally** as Christ loves us, we refrain from making quick judgments, stereotyping, and drawing conclusions. Rather than seeing others as competition with whom we are vying for the good things, we can share the rewards and blessings of this life.

Through **forgiving others** as we have been forgiven, we exhibit a level of spiritual maturity and transformation that brings about peace, reconciliation, and healing. Being aware of our own sins reminds us to be more patient with others who, like ourselves, are a work in progress.

Through **serving others**, we give generously of our time and talents for the building up of the kingdom. Helping the poor, sick, and marginalized is what Jesus taught us to do by his example. We can show up to serve at the homeless center, bring meals to those who are grieving or laid up, or be an activist for justice.

Through **praying for others**, not only when they are sick or grieving, but also through their everyday struggles, we show our love and concern. Letting others know we are praying, and being faithful in lifting those prayers to heaven can be a genuine source of encouragement during difficult times.

Through **sharing the good news** of salvation, our friends, neighbors, and coworkers will take notice. This might mean stepping out of our comfort zones as we share our faith in situations where it may not be welcome.

As we "grow up" in our faith, the outward signs of love, forgiveness, service, prayer, and sharing the gospel will help others see Christ through us, and God will be glorified.

 *Take notice*

When you use a measuring device today (e.g. a ruler, scale, measuring cup, or thermometer), identify one way you've grown (or wish to grow) spiritually. How can others see this growth?

Prayer

Dear Lord, may others see your love through me today and every day. Amen.

thursday

Front porch people

No one who conceals transgressions will prosper, but one
who confesses and forsakes them will obtain mercy.
Proverbs 28:13

I miss the days of front-porch-sitting.

Even though I didn't grow up with a front porch, when I read books like *To Kill a Mockingbird* and others that romanticize the front porch, I miss those days.

Blame it on air-conditioning. Or busyness. Or screens (and no, I'm not talking about the kind that keeps the bugs away). The fact is, today we rarely see folks sipping lemonade and fanning themselves on their front porch as they chat and wave to passersby.

As I drive, walk, or ride my bike past nearby homes, I see closed doors. Curtained windows. Privacy fences. And big, beautiful, *empty* front porches. I am guilty myself of leaving my own front porch to gather dust.

We often know nothing of the people that live nearby, yet they are our neighbors, our community. In the front-porch-sitting days, we would have known each other on a first-name basis.

But where has everyone gone? And why are we hiding?

We have become a society of isolation and fear. We build fences to block out the noise of the world, protect our children, and keep strangers out. In fear of exposing ourselves, we avoid eye contact and prefer to close our windows and doors.

We keep ourselves hidden.

Yet, if we don't open ourselves up to those around us, we might shut out Jesus. In his Word, he tells us to forgive one another, to carry one another's burdens, to fellowship together, and to pray for one another. But we can't do that for each other, or know how to do that, if we're not willing to open up and share our needs.

When we become vulnerable–sharing our struggles, our fears, and our weaknesses–Jesus shows up. If we call on him, he will be there in our time of need. His mercy is also accessible through the neighbors and friends who love and accept us, forgive us despite the failings we want to hide, and pray for us in our struggles.

If we just open the door and step out onto the "porch" of openness and honesty, we will find our fears to be unfounded.

Our insecurities met with acceptance. Our vulnerability rewarded with friendship and affirmation.

We will find the love of Jesus.

Take notice

When you're out and about today, use the front porches you see as a reminder that Jesus is calling you to step out onto yours by sharing deeply with others.

Prayer

Dear Jesus, thank you for accepting me with all my faults and fears. Bring others into my life who will show me your love, grace, and mercy. Amen.

friday

Grumpiness

Therefore, as God's chosen ones, holy and beloved, clothe
yourselves with compassion, kindness, humility, meekness,
and patience. Bear with one another and, if anyone has a
complaint against another, forgive each other; just as the
Lord has forgiven you, so you also must forgive.
Colossians 3:12-13

My husband used to joke that he wanted to live to be 100 so he could be a "grumpy old man." Now here we are, over half-way to his goal of being centenarians. We can also be pretty grumpy. (You don't want to talk to me before I've had my morning coffee.)

I've heard others say, and often thought to myself, that the elderly can be inflexible. I've seen it in myself. When things are out of sync in my routine, I can become irritable and even rude. If I sense the slightest bit of unfairness–whether it's how long I spend doing the dishes, my volunteer hours at church, or someone taking too long in the checkout line at the store–I sulk, become impatient, and get angry with the world.

But it's not just the elderly. I see it in the younger generation as well. We all have a case of the "me firsts." A sense of entitlement. A plague brought on by the sins of self-centeredness, greed, and lack of gratitude that infest our "me-first" culture.

Thankfully, I've also had first-hand experience with the flip side. As I cared for my mother during her final months on this earth, her kindness, patience, and contentment moved me. She rarely complained (though she had many reasons to) and never stopped being concerned for others. Even though she was bedridden, she would ask, "Do you need anything?" If she could have gotten out of that bed, she would have walked to the kitchen and put the teapot on and insisted I sit down. Serving others and putting them first was her way.

I remember attending a class on marriage once where husbands and wives were challenged to out-serve each other. It humbled me, and I had to admit I more often looked to be served than to serve; to have kindness shown to me, rather than to show kindness.

We all fall short on the kindness meter from time to time. But Paul's letter to the Colossians reminds us to forgive, and also that we have been forgiven. *"Forgive as quickly and completely as the Master forgave you."* (Col 3:13b, MSG).

Through forgiveness, we have the chance to start over with each new minute, hour, or day.

In today's angsty society, there are plenty of reasons to be grumpy, critical, and impatient. Instead, let's seek opportunities to be kind, understanding, and accepting.

The choice is ours.

Take notice

When tempted into grumpiness (i.e. impatience, irritability, unkindness) today, focus on forgiveness–of others and yourself–instead, and replace your grumpiness with gratitude.

Prayer

Lord Jesus, help me clothe myself today with compassion, kindness, humility, gentleness, and patience. Amen.

saturday

(don't) Spare me the details

For I am not ashamed of the gospel; it is God's saving power for everyone who believes, for the Jew first and also for the Greek. Romans 1:16

My husband says I got my story-telling skills from my mom. And I've passed them on to my youngest daughter. We can't tell a story without including every detail. Someone might miss the point if we don't include what we were eating for dinner–including the spiciness of the salsa–when we tell them how the phone rang and it was our sister who told us all about her exciting adventure on the way to picking up her kids from their basketball practice, which overlapped with her other kid's dentist appointment... (my sister inherited the same story-telling skills).

The details build the story up. They create suspense. They help my listener picture the events more clearly. Right? I know, I know. I can go overboard sometimes.

I try not to monopolize the conversation. I look for signs that I'm boring my listener, like they're looking at their watch, squirming in their seat, or inching for the door. When I see those signs, I wrap things up as quickly as I can. A lot of what I say really isn't that important, so "cut to the chase," I tell myself, "spare them the details."

But sometimes, the story just won't be satisfied until it's told *with* all the details. The story is just too good to keep inside.

That's how I want to feel about the Gospel. After his resurrection, Jesus told his disciples to *"Go into all the world and proclaim the good news to the whole creation."* (Mark 16:15) That good news is the story of salvation. And it's a story that's just too good to keep to ourselves.

Do we have a sense of urgency to tell *that* story? The details go back to the Garden of Eden, Adam and Eve, and the Fall of the human race. The story wanders through the wilderness with God's people throughout the Old Testament, through their disobedience, repentance, and God's unrelenting love for them, a love that promised a Messiah would come to save His people once and for all. That Messiah came as a baby, powerless and poor, yet grew into a man with God's power to heal the sick and raise the dead. A man who loved the poor, preached mercy, and forgave sins.

This story is too good to cut short. But it's also difficult to explain. How this man, God's Son, who showed nothing but love and mercy, was beaten and bruised and nailed to a cross. How he died there for our sins.

He was laid in the tomb, and the stone sealed the story inside. But the story doesn't end there. It's a story that's just too good to keep inside.

Stay tuned for the end of the story with *all* of its glorious details, on Easter Sunday.

Take notice

Tell someone a story today. Remember the greatest story ever told, and if you know it well, ask God to give you opportunities to share it.

Prayer

Lord, thank you for making your story my story. Give me the courage, desire, and opportunity to share that story with others. Amen.

week seven:

Holy Week

monday

Calendars

Jesus Christ is the same yesterday and today and forever.
Hebrews 13:8

What kind of calendar do you use? I prefer a digital calendar that syncs up my laptop and my phone. It detects dates in my email and texts, and plunks them into my calendar with little effort on my part. With a few clicks, it automatically enters repeating events and sends me reminders when I request them.

I know others who swear by their Franklin planner. Or their bullet journal. Some busy families use a big whiteboard wall calendar to track everybody's comings and goings. Before my mom got Alzheimer's, she used a simple paper calendar—one of those freebies you get in the mail from charitable organizations—to track her children's and grandchildren's birthdays and anniversaries, as well as her and Dad's doctor visits, hair appointments, and church meetings.

Whichever calendar you prefer, it's safe to say you use one. Doing so not only helps us remember events that have transpired in the past. It also prepares us to look forward toward what is coming next.

The church calendar is similar. It moves in a circle from one season of the church year to the next. It prompts us to remember the special holy days of Christmas, Epiphany, Easter, and Pentecost, while giving us preparatory seasons of Advent and Lent, and "ordinary" time in between. Like our everyday calendars, the church calendar was created by humans to be used as a tool—one that has been used for centuries.

Even though humans invented these means of tracking time, it is God who created the gift of time itself. He's also given us the ability to look back, to plan ahead, and to be in the present moment, each of which is valuable.

One tool I've used to reflect on a day, week, or season is the "Examen" prayer. If the term is new to you, don't let the Latin word, or that it sounds like an "exam," turn you off. It's really quite simple.

The Examen is a prayer framework that helps us bring the events on our calendars, as well as spontaneous moments in time, into focus. A key part of the Examen is to review the time that has passed by reflecting on what has brought you joy and where you have struggled. In bringing these thoughts before the Lord, we can find peace through giving thanks, seeking help, and noticing God's presence in our lives. The prayer practice ends by looking forward and asking the Spirit to guide your next steps.

Whether your calendar's days are scheduled from morning to night or wearily empty, our Heavenly Father is at work. If turning back the pages of your calendar brings joy, sadness, peace, or regret, Jesus–who took on our humanity– can relate. If the future stirs up anxiety or excitement, the Holy Spirit will be there with you.

He was there in our yesterdays. He'll be there in our tomorrows.

Let's reach out to him today.

 Take notice

When you open your calendar today, add this entry: Spend time with Jesus. Then make sure you keep your appointment! To enrich this time, use the framework of the Examen prayer. (JesuitResource.org provides helpful prompts.)

 Prayer

Dear Jesus, thank you for the days, weeks, months, and years; for the gifts of seasons, of calendars, and of time. Remind me to fill all my days with your presence. Amen.

tuesday

Blood Red

In him we have redemption through his blood, the forgiveness of our trespasses, according to the riches of his grace that he lavished on us. Ephesians 1:7-8a

Nothing but the blood of Jesus.

It's strange to sing about blood. But when we sing the old hymn *Nothing But the Blood of Jesus*, we do just that. It's Jesus' blood that was shed on the cross for the forgiveness of our sins. But do we really think about what that means? Do we imagine the streams of red pouring from his side and hands and feet? Can we fathom his suffering?

In my world of modern-day comforts, I'll admit, it's hard. I lose a drop of blood from a paper cut and grab a band-aid.

When one of my children had a bloody nose or scraped a knee, I rushed to stop the bleeding.

Jesus' blood was poured out for us. Red, red rivers bringing salvation and forgiveness for the wrongs we do every day. Again, it's hard to fathom.

And so, as we enter this most sacred and Holy week, we will find reminders. As we have used other common objects in our surroundings, this week, we will look for the color red.

Dark red, wine-colored leaves still clinging to the bushes and trees from a season that has passed.

Red flags on the mailboxes that alert the mail carrier to stop, and the octagon signs that remind us to STOP, look, and listen.

A red cardinal, bright against a freshly green backdrop, ready to usher in spring and its new life.

When we see red, we will remember Jesus' blood, shed for us.

What can wash away my sin?
What can make me whole again?
Nothing but the blood of Jesus.

For my pardon this I see…
For my cleansing this my plea:
Nothing but the blood of Jesus.

Nothing can for sin atone…
Naught of good that I have done,
Nothing but the blood of Jesus.

O precious is the flow
That makes me white as snow;
No other fount I know;
Nothing but the blood of Jesus

This is all my hope and peace…
This is all my righteousness:
Nothing but the blood of Jesus.
(Robert Lowry, 1876)

Take notice

When you see the color red today, pause for a moment.
Remember the blood of Jesus that was shed for your sins.

Prayer

Jesus, thank you for washing away my sins with your
precious blood. Help me live for you. Amen.

wednesday

the Path

For to this you have been called, because Christ also suffered for you, leaving you an example, so that you should follow in his steps. 1 Peter 2:21

I was hiking a trail through the woods. And I wondered, where did this path come from?

If one person walks through the woods or a meadow, no path is formed. But if many others follow, the grass is beaten down, the brush pushed aside, and a path forms. Or, if one person takes the same steps day after day, soon, a trail is marked.

It's the repetition and the following that enables us to see the path so we can repeat and follow as well.

In days gone by, there were only footpaths. Then smaller trails became wider as more people used them. Then horses took those paths. Later, horses pulled buggies, and the trail became a road. Then cars came along. And pavement. Then came bigger cars and trucks. Finally, the way from point A to point B became a superhighway with at least three lanes in either direction and vehicles speeding by at 70 mph.

Highways make it easy to get from here to there. But in our Lenten journey, Jesus asks us to take the road less traveled. He walked the Via Dolorosa, the Way of Sorrows, as he carried his cross to Calvary. Sacrificing everything, he walked this agonizing path for us.

Since then, many have walked in Jesus' footsteps by taking up their own crosses–making sacrifices in their lives–and giving Jesus their everything. They've asked "What would Jesus do?" when faced with questions of love and mercy. Jesus' disciples, ancient teachers and preachers, and the saints of old repeated his teachings and followed in his footsteps of sacrifice and mercy. They also made a path for us to follow.

Are we willing to walk this road with Jesus? He told us it wouldn't be an easy, superhighway kind of road. In fact, he said, *"Enter through the narrow gate, for the gate is wide and the road is easy that leads to destruction, and there are many who take it. For the gate is narrow, and the road is hard that leads to life, and there are few who find it."* (Matt. 7:13-14)

The road may not be easy, but Jesus made it possible. He cleared the way. Now he calls us to come to him. And when we lose our footing, or the path is steep and difficult, he will walk beside us. He knows our pain and suffering.

If we follow him, he will guide us through.

Take notice

When walking a path or taking a road or highway today, meditate for a minute on the path that Jesus walked. Consider his suffering. Are you willing to suffer too?

Prayer

Dear Jesus, Thank you for suffering and dying for me. Give me the desire to give my life to you and sacrifice my all for you. Amen.

Maundy thursday

Dirty feet

Jesus said, "If I don't wash you, you can't be part of what I'm doing." John 13:8b (MSG)

It's a warm spring day, and I can't wait to get outside and do a little garden cleanup. I slip my bare feet into my light blue plastic Crocs and head outside. My meager tulips and daffodils are showing their colors. One of my garden's more recent highlights–my Lenten rose–is aware of the season and blooming in perfectly pink-edged white petals.

As I pull early spring weeds and prune a few bushes, I notice my mulch needs replenishing. The ground surrounding my plants has become mostly dirt at this point in the year.

Once back in the house, I realize it would have been wise to put on socks and more protective footwear. The soles of my feet are dusty and brown. I tiptoe to the bathroom to avoid making tracks through the house and begin the messy task of washing my dirty feet.

Today is Maundy Thursday. It's the day we remember Jesus' last supper with his disciples. Many churches will meet and remember this holy day by celebrating communion together. Perhaps you will attend a gathering at your own house of worship.

But did you know that the word "maundy" refers to that moment before Jesus' last supper when he washed his disciples' feet?

As was the custom in Jesus' day, a guest would have their feet washed when entering a house. Like the Crocs over my bare feet, the sandals the disciples wore didn't keep the dirt out. In Jesus' day, there were no paved roads or sidewalks and no Nike tennis shoes. People's feet were pretty disgusting by the end of the day. When a host offered to have their guests' feet washed as they entered the house, it showed care and a warm welcome. It was a sign of hospitality.

Since servants were typically the ones washing dirty feet, some disciples objected to their Lord–the son of God– stooping down to wash their feet. By washing his disciples' feet, Jesus was not only modeling humility but also symbolizing the washing away of sins that he was about to accomplish through his death on the cross.

When Peter objected, Jesus said, *"Unless I wash you, you have no share with me."* Then Peter said: *"Lord, not my feet only but also my hands and my head!"* (John 13: 8b-9).

Jesus' actions that day were a teaching moment. And they include a lesson for us too. Not only does Jesus command us to *"eat, drink, remember, and believe"* when we take communion, but he also shows us how we are to live in community with others.

By showing love and care in our actions and words, we welcome our friends and neighbors into the family of God with *hospitality*.

By serving others with *humility*, we mirror the servant nature of Christ.

And by offering *forgiveness* to others, we acknowledge our own need for forgiveness through Christ's sacrificial death.

 Take notice

Wash your feet (or wash something for someone else) today, and remember the symbol of Christ's hospitality, humility, and forgiveness.

🙏 Prayer

Lord Jesus, give me opportunities to be like you in caring for, serving, and forgiving others. Amen.

Good Friday

Walking through Darkness

Again Jesus spoke to them, saying, "I am the light of the world. Whoever follows me will never walk in darkness but will have the light of life." John 8:12

Recently, my husband and I did some remodeling in our home, which included an update of our master bedroom. We replaced the frayed, old comforter with a smart, new quilt. The smashed, worn carpet was ousted for a mottled plush that felt like clouds under my bare toes.

The biggest change to our bedroom decor was the furniture. While our old dresser, chest, and nightstands were solid and well made, it was time for the honey oak finish and country-style hardware to go. Rather than invest in new pieces, however, we opted to hire a painter to refinish what we already owned.

After living out of clothes baskets for several weeks, finally the day came to bring the newly painted pieces back home. To mix things up a little more, we swapped my dresser's position with my husband's chest of drawers. The end result was lovely.

That is, until the middle of the night, when I got up to go to the bathroom. In the darkness, I couldn't see (and didn't remember) there was now a long dresser where once there had been a tall chest. The corner jutted out into my path, bringing a sharp pain to the side of my hip. The "ouch!" was loud enough to wake my husband, and the bruise that followed was an ugly reminder of the dangers that lurk in the darkness.

On this most somber day in the church calendar year, we enter a much deeper darkness with Jesus. His friends have deserted him. The people who one week earlier had lined his path with palm branches and "Hosannas!" have turned against him as well. The pain he endures on his way to Calvary and in his death on the cross makes him feel forgotten and forsaken even by his Heavenly Father.

Why do we remember and relive this pain year after year on Good Friday? Why not just bring this story up now and again like the story of Noah's ark or Jonah in the whale's belly?

We must retell this story of deepest darkness. It's the cornerstone on which our faith stands and the door to the way of salvation.

Since that night when I bumped my hip, I've developed a new habit when walking to the bathroom in the dark. Every time I walk by, I reach out my hand and touch the corner of the dresser. Doing so reminds me of what is there, helps me find my way safely, and saves me from the pain I once felt.

As we walk through the darkness of this crucifixion night, let us bend our hearts toward heaven and remember Jesus' sacrifice. Let us hear his cries and, in our imaginations, reach out our hands to touch the corner of the wooden cross on which he's nailed.

As we remember, let us find our way through the darkness to the One who saves us and brings us safely through the night.

 *Take notice*

During the dark hours of this day, reach out and find a guide—a doorway, a wall, or a piece of furniture. Use that moment as a reminder that Jesus suffered and died so that you would never walk in darkness again.

Prayer

Jesus, my salvation, you gave your life so that I could always walk in the light. I give you my life in return. Amen.

Holy saturday

Filling our baskets

You show me the path of life.
In your presence there is fullness of joy;
in your right hand are pleasures forevermore. Psalm 16:11

When my children were young, despite my desire to simplify, getting ready for Easter was always a production. Anticipating some family pictures, I'd buy new dress shirts for the boys that coordinated with the girls' frilly spring dresses. Of course, there was always the last-minute discovery that the boys' dress pants from last year were two inches too short and the girls' white tights had holes in them, and I'd run off to the store again. In addition to our spring wardrobe, I also spent time buying and prepping food for

Easter dinner, and sometimes packing overnight bags for our family's stay at Grandpa and Grandma's house. Many years, Easter fell right around our anniversary and two of my children's birthdays, which just added more things to prepare for and do.

Getting ready was exhausting. On Saturday night, after the kids were finally bathed and in bed, my husband and I would complete one last task of filling the Easter baskets for our kids to find the next morning. There were chocolate eggs and bunnies and enough jelly beans to fill several plastic eggs. We added a couple of special gifts: something fun–a stuffed bunny, bubbles, yo-yos, or sidewalk chalk; and something meaningful–a children's Bible, Veggie Tales movie, cross necklace, or Christian music CD.

Despite my lack of sleep, seeing their wide eyes as they approached the baskets the next morning and the pure joy on their faces as they dug through the plastic grass to find their treasures was worth it all.

Since I no longer need to dress our clan to the nines or fill four brimming Easter baskets, I'm looking instead for ways to prepare my heart for Easter.

Holy Saturday, that time of waiting between Jesus' crucifixion on Good Friday and his resurrection on Easter morning, is the perfect time to reflect on our journey through Lent.

We've been reminded of Jesus' presence in the everyday things that surround us. Our mirrors, the bank, evergreen trees, power lines, and even our own grumpiness or dirty feet, are just some of the ways we've found Jesus in the world around us.

These moments spent with Jesus over the past 40 days are the treasures we can use to fill our own baskets. We've been storing up our encounters with Jesus in anticipation of great joy. On Easter morning, as we open our sleepy eyes, we will be like children, expectant and giddy. Our baskets, filled with answered prayers of forgiveness, love, joy, grace, and mercy, are brimming and waiting for us to receive them.

This season's journey to the cross with Jesus culminates in one glorious day!

But our journey never ends.

Our walk with him continues. Day by day, hour by hour, minute by minute...we will find him by our side. We only need to open our eyes to his presence and our ears to his calling. Our friend–the Savior of the world–will never leave us.

Take notice

As you look back over the past 40 days, recall the ways that Jesus was most present to you. Perhaps you found him in one of the everyday practices you were given here, or you discovered another means on your own. Maybe there are no specific memories, but you found a general sense of Jesus' presence simply by taking time to think about him and say a prayer each day. Whatever treasures you have found, gather them in your "Easter basket" and bring them with joy to your house of worship tomorrow.

Prayer

God Almighty, Lord Jesus, Holy Spirit–I lift up my heart in praise to you. I thank you for being ever present with me, for taking my sins to the cross, and for conquering death. I pray that I will continue to seek and find you, all the days of my life. Amen.

Easter Sunday

If the Spirit of him who raised Jesus from the dead dwells in you, he who raised Christ Jesus from the dead will give life to your mortal bodies also through his Spirit that dwells in you.
Romans 8:11

Jesus is risen!!

He is risen indeed!!

Alleluia!!

About the author

Linda Hanstra, a semi-retired speech-language pathologist, lives with her husband, Tom, in southwest Michigan and spends summers in Northern Minnesota–their home away from home. Cruising along on their "empty-nest joyride," they have four adult children, a daughter-in-love, and (at the time of this writing) one adorable grandson.

Linda has been a member of the Christian Reformed Church in South Bend, Indiana, for over 35 years. She has recently served as elder, praise team member, and children's worship leader.

You can visit her at www.lindahanstra.com and on Substack at lindahanstra.substack.com where she writes about faith, family, lake life, cycling, travel, and empty-nesting.

Acknowledgments

So many have encouraged me on this Journey. Thank you.

To Tom, for your patience and love. For getting up early and bringing me coffee. For supporting me in giving up my day job, so I could finally finish something I started. I love you.

To Jared, Seth & Maddie, Leah, and Chloe, for all you've taught me and the joy you've brought me. And to Ollie, for making me laugh.

To my sisters, Phyllis, Barb, Beth, and Diane (and to brother Jon too!), for sister weekends, memories, laughter and tears. Thanks for believing in me.

To my nieces Shanna and Sandra, for the design help, marketing advice, and tech hints that pulled this project together.

To Mary V., for your willingness to look at my work before it goes out into the world, for your sage advice, and most of all, for your friendship over the years.

To Jessica T., for your generosity, astute attention to detail, and kind words that gave me the confidence to move forward.

To Christina R., for giving your time and wisdom, and for your ability to gently steer me in the right direction.

To Linda C., for keeping me accountable in my writing goals and to my spiritual calling; you're a great teacher, writer, and friend.

To Callie F, for starting me on my writing journey and for first suggesting I might have a book in me.

And to my faithful readers, for encouraging me along the way; you kept me going when I wasn't even sure where I was headed.

Notes:

Notes:

Notes:

Notes: